FATHER OF THE CONSTITUTION

A Creative Minds Biography

FATHER OF THE CONSTITUTION

A Story about James Madison

by Barbara Mitchell

illustrations by Alex Tavoularis

Carolrhoda Books, Inc./Minneapolis

For Michael Helman
and the Chancel Ringers —B.J.M.

Text copyright © 2004 by Barbara Mitchell
Illustrations copyright © 2004 by Alex Tavoularis

This book is available in two editions:
Library binding by Carolrhoda Books, Inc.
    a division of Lerner Publishing Group
Soft cover by First Avenue Editions
    an imprint of Lerner Publishing Group
241 First Avenue North
Minneapolis, MN 55401 U.S.A.

Website address: www.lernerbooks.com

Library of Congress Cataloging-in-Publication Data

Mitchell, Barbara, 1941–
    Father of the Constitution: a story about James Madison / by Barbara
Mitchell ; illustrations by Alex Tavoularis.
        p.   cm. — (A creative minds biography)
    Summary: Introduces the life of President James Madison, focusing on
his life-long interest in books and study, as well as his role as "Father of
the Constitution" and historian of the Constitutional Convention.
    Includes bibliographical references and index.
    ISBN: 1-57505-182-6 (lib. bdg. : alk. paper)
    ISBN: 1-57505-607-0 (pbk. : alk. paper)
    1. Madison, James, 1751–1836—Juvenile literature. 2. Presidents—
United States—Biography—Juvenile literature. [1. Madison, James,
1751–1836. 2. Presidents.] I. Tavoularis, Alex, ill. II. Title. III. Series.
E342.M58 2004
973.5'1'092—dc21   2002152918

Manufactured in the United States of America
1 2 3 4 5 6 – JR – 09 08 07 06 05 04

Table of Contents

1

Louder, Madison

All his life, James Madison would remember the year that he was nine. That was the year he moved from Grandmother's place up to the big brick house. Father had let him help carry furniture.

It was the year George III became king of Great Britain. As the new king was leaving his coronation ceremony, a large jewel had suddenly fallen from his crown to the steps of Westminster Abbey, where British kings and queens were crowned. People in the crowd outside the stately church murmured that the fallen jewel was an omen. King George would lose a chunk of his kingdom.

Nine-year-old "Jemmy" (the name James Madison Sr. called his firstborn son) had no way of knowing that one day he would be part of King George's story. He was just a boy living in the colony of Virginia, on the other side of the Atlantic Ocean. He knew he was British, of course. All the people of Virginia were British.

Jemmy knew how the Madison land had been granted to his ancestors long ago by an English king. He knew how Grandfather's slaves had built their house from trees in the Madison forest, how he had planted tobacco in the rich, orange Virginia soil. He knew how Grandmother had managed the 2,850–acre plantation herself after Grandfather had died. She had raised her three children, seen to the welfare of twenty-nine Madison slaves, and shipped the Madison tobacco to Great Britain. Grandmother told Jemmy stories about these things.

There was something Jemmy noticed about Grandmother's stories. There were holes. What had life for the Madison family been like back in Britain? Jemmy wanted to know. His ancestors had been planters, Grandmother told him. The rest of the story was history lost forever. No one had written it down.

Grandmother Madison loved history, and she loved literature. With all her busyness, Frances Madison had found time to read good books. She wanted

Jemmy to love these things too. Grandmother read aloud from *The Spectator*. The set of eight books was special. She had ordered them from Great Britain when Jemmy was just one year old. The books were filled with essays, commentaries on life and how it might be lived to the fullest. *The Spectator* writers were thinkers, Grandmother said. Perhaps Jemmy would be a writer and a thinker as well.

One day Jemmy had a surprise for his grandmother. He could read *The Spectator* to her, he announced. Not only that, but he had been reading the twenty-eight books on Grandfather's shelf. Grandmother was amazed—her Jemmy was reading books written for grown-ups. It seemed only yesterday that she and his mother had helped him sound out words in *The Grand and Glorious Adventures of Reynard the Fox,* a children's storybook.

But the most wonderful surprise of all that year of 1760, when Jemmy Madison was nine, came on moving day. That day Jemmy helped carry the furniture into the big, new house a quarter mile up the road. Making its way into Father's tall walnut bookcases was a grand procession of eighty-five books. Father actually owned that many books!

Father liked books on curiosities, such as the one about the strange little animals that squirmed under an invention called a microscope and the book on how to take a cold bath. There was a curiosity! Although it was said that the royal governor down in Williamsburg actually sat naked in a bathing house while a servant poured cold water over him, most Virginians simply sponged off.

Nelly Madison was not in favor of her delicate eldest son dousing himself with ice water. Bathing was believed to wash away nature's protective oils. Jemmy was sick a lot as it was. He had seizures that caused him to suddenly lose control over his body. Jemmy called this "the falling sickness." He was small for his age and had a voice as wispy as the wind. Mother's most used book was *The Compleat Virginia Housewife.* Mother was forever looking up remedies for fever and stomach complaint.

Never mind. There was always a good book to help the situation. If the weather was fine, Jemmy might carry his book to the porch facing the magnificent Blue Ridge Mountains. There, he might find a refreshing breeze to rustle the pages. When raindrops pattered the new glass windows, there was the crackling fire in the new parlor, with Father's *Country Gentlemen* magazines nearby. Reading! Jemmy loved it. By the time he was eleven, he had read every book and magazine in the house.

A teacher named Donald Robertson was setting up school on a plantation in neighboring King and Queen County. Robertson was known to be one of the finest schoolmasters in all the thirteen colonies. The Madisons arranged for their book-loving son to attend. But Jemmy was not so sure that he wanted to go. The school was on a plantation seventy miles from home. He would have to stay with the plantation owner's family. Other than a sprinkling of Madison cousins, he would not know one boy in the class. Jemmy was shy.

He did go, though, and he soon had something happy to write home about. The schoolmaster had a library that would have caused Grandmother Madison to smile. (Grandmother had passed away not long after the move to the new house.) The library was full of history books, stories about ancient Greece and Rome and their thinkers. The Greeks called their thinkers philosophers, Jemmy learned. The philosophers—Plato, Aristotle, and Socrates—asked questions nobody else had even thought of.

That is just what Master Robertson expected his young scholars to do. Most colonial schoolmasters simply gave out facts. The students spit the facts back word for word. But a Robertson student was a thinking student.

For the first year, Jemmy developed his thinking skills in English. Then it was on to Latin, the scholar's language. Robertson showed that close to half the English language had grown out of this language of ancient Rome. Knowing a word's original meaning made its meaning in English absolutely clear, Jemmy learned. Next came Latin grammar, the parts of speech, all laid out in neat little columns according to how they might be used to create clear sentences.

Jemmy was soon handling language precisely. Mr. Robertson was a stickler for his students thinking, writing, and speaking with precision. Jemmy had a talent for reasoning. He turned out essays as clear as a Blue Ridge Mountain stream. It was the speaking part that troubled him.

"LOUDER, MADISON," Master Robertson urged, when it was Jemmy's turn to read to the class from Virgil, the great Roman poet. Publius Virgilius. Jemmy loved the very sound of the poet's name. But he could not bring himself to speak up in class. It was that wispy little voice of his, he told his teacher.

"Madison?" Master Robertson encouraged when a question hung heavy in the air. Jemmy never raised his hand. There were interesting questions to be posed. What, for example, did the lads think of King George's new Stamp Act? The king had declared a tax on printed material in his American colonies. Everything but books and personal letters must bear the expensive stamp of King George.

Hands shot up. Why must the colonists buy a tax stamp simply to read a newspaper? Why must a lawyer pay as much as ten English pounds to file a legal paper? Why was there a tax on an advertisement of a horse for sale? Why must there be a tax on a deck of playing cards?

The Madison boy was well acquainted with tax talk. Mr. Robertson knew that for a fact. The new house at the foothills of the Blue Ridge Mountains was a gathering spot for lawyers and politicians all over Orange County. There were answers shining in those bright eyes. "SAY IT, MADISON." But Jemmy Madison said not a word.

Then the Reverend Thomas Martin came to board with the Madison family, and Father decided Jemmy should continue his education at home with the new minister. The leave-taking presented Mr. Robertson with a question of his own. Would the boy from Orange County ever make use of his talents? More than a weak voice was troubling this outstanding student he had worked with for five years. It was shyness, crippling shyness. Only Jemmy Madison himself could conquer that.

2

Politics and Pots of Tea

Home was different when teenaged James returned. Mother kept the tea caddy locked so the precious contents would not be stolen. Finishing touches on the new house were at a standstill. Summer barbecues buzzed with talk of King George. Since when could this new king set their taxes? Virginians asked. It was the landowners, such as James Madison Sr., who had always had the power to vote on laws for Virginia.

A fiery lawmaker named Patrick Henry had dared to speak to the Virginia legislature. The people in Great Britain had a say in their taxes, Henry roared. They had representatives in King George's British government. The colonists were British. But they had not one representative. They should put up a squawk, that's what.

Squawk the colonists did. It was enough to make King George's powdered wig stand on end. Allow those naughty colonists a representative? Indeed not. From now on, there would be tax on building supplies—the lead, glass, and paint used in those fancy colonial houses—arriving on British ships. And yes, he would place a tax on tea.

The colonists were angry. A tax on tea? Why, King George jerked them around as though they were babies on leading strings. (Colonial toddlers had strings attached to their dresses, lest they stray too far from their parents.)

When he was not listening in on angry political talk, James studied Greek with the Reverend Martin, his new tutor. Greek was a requirement for entrance to the College of New Jersey at Princeton. Martin was a Princeton graduate. At his school, he boasted, students were encouraged to have a spirit of freedom.

Most Virginians who had college-bound sons sent them to the College of William and Mary in Williamsburg. The Madisons were patriots—supporters of the colonists' side of the squabbles with King George. Would they send their son to a college right under the royal governor's nose? No! Princeton it would be.

James set out for New Jersey in early summer 1769, accompanied by the Reverend Martin and a slave named Sawney. Across Virginia they rode, on through Maryland, and up into Delaware. At last they reached Philadelphia, Pennsylvania. Philadelphia was the largest and most beautiful city in the colonies. Cobblestone streets glimmered with 662 whale-oil lamps, and the beautiful State House, where Pennsylvania's lawmakers met, stood grandly over it all.

The little group would stop by the London Coffeehouse before crossing the river to New Jersey, said Martin. There was more than coffee brewing at this popular stop for travelers. The owner was a printer. Served up with the famous Philadelphia sticky buns were pamphlets hot off the Bradford press, anti-British pamphlets.

William Bradford, the printer's son, was also Princeton bound, James learned. It was not long before he and William were best friends. As often as they could, James and William rented horses and rode down to Philadelphia. The forty-mile journey took the better part of a day if they hurried. The trip was well worthwhile.

In Philadelphia they listened to the coffeehouse talk. They bought all seven Philadelphia newspapers. Armed with the latest in political news and gossip, they prepared for gatherings of the Whigs, a patriots' club formed with nine other students. The purpose of club meetings was to read essays, discuss, and debate. Half of the students would take King George's side of an argument. The other half took the colonists' side. Dr. John Witherspoon, the new college president, gave his approval. The battles encouraged freedom of thought. The talk would go far into the night, until at last Witherspoon rapped at the door, with "Enough, lads, enough."

Rules were strict at Princeton. There was to be no "coddling with dainties," spoiling with sweet treats. However, young gentlemen who had shown themselves to be serious about their studies were permitted a cup of tea in their rooms during philosophical debates. Soon even lofty seniors were hugging steaming cups of tea, their ears tuned in to James Madison.

Madison knew more than anyone on campus about the ancient Greeks and their experimental government called democracy, a government ruled by the people themselves. That was just what the young patriots wanted to hear. James had no trouble at all talking before this little group of friends, especially since the discussions centered on how government worked. Government and political history were his favorite college subjects.

The subject considered vitally important at Princeton, though, was public speaking. The school had been established for training ministers. It was also known for graduating outstanding lawyers. Every student was required to "declaim," to present either a selection from literature or a piece of his own persuasive writing in assembly every week. The powerful voices of future preachers and lawyers pounded Nassau Hall.

James Madison sat rigid in his chair, dreading the awful moment he would be called upon to declaim. Not that he wasn't prepared. James devoured literature from Princeton's two-thousand-book library like a kitten lapping cream. He had filled an entire notebook on how to present foolproof arguments.

Each week the moment arrived. Stomach fluttering, his head as light as a hot air balloon, James walked to the speaker's stand. Sweat trickled down his ruffled collar. His breathing came shallow in his chest. Suppose he should have an attack of the old "falling sickness" and faint dead away! The thought of speaking in front of the entire student body left James Madison absolutely terrified.

Despite his difficulty with public speaking, James was graduated with honors. It was time he put that expensive education to use, said Father. The problem was that James had not the slightest idea of what he wanted to do, what he should be.

He could begin by teaching his school-age brothers and sisters, Father said. (Altogether, James had eleven brothers and sisters. Five of them had died in childhood.) Dutifully, James put in his teaching hours, but he felt no calling to this profession, he said.

So Mr. Madison took his son to observe at Culpepper County Courthouse. Perhaps James would feel inspired to enter law. The idea of reading English law books all day was equally unappealing to the young patriot. But as they were leaving, a minister was declaiming, preaching his heart out, from a jailhouse window. Half a dozen Baptist preachers were in Culpepper County's jail for offenses as simple as offering prayer in a home or baptizing in a river. According to English law, such things could take place only inside the local Anglican Church, the Church of England.

Depression settled over James Madison like a blanket of mountain fog. He missed his college friends, the lively debates over cups of tea. The decision of what to do with life nagged at him. Perhaps his good friend should consider going into politics, William

Bradford wrote. I DO NOT MEDDLE IN POLI-TICS, James fired back.

Christmas was coming. There would be no tea from King George's ships served this Christmastime of 1773. The British Parliament had passed the Tea Act. The new law actually lowered the price of tea that was shipped to the colonies, but it did not take away the tea tax.

The British thought the Americans were sure to buy the cheap tea and stop complaining about taxation without representation. But the patriotic ladies of Virginia and the other colonies were not fooled. Liberty tea, brewed from peppermint and raspberries out of their own American backyards would do just fine.

In the midst of the Christmas festivities, a greeting arrived from William Bradford. A most alarming event had occurred, William reported. Colonists in Boston had boarded three British ships. They had dumped the cargo, ninety thousand pounds of tea, into icy Boston Harbor. Something big was going on. Perhaps he and James should plan to meet in Philadelphia and talk it all over.

James made his visit in the spring. Friday the thirteenth was unlucky for sure that May of 1774. A messenger on horseback dashed into the city. King George had closed of the port of Boston. It was a punishment for what Boston called the "Tea Party." King George called it treason. On Saturday morning, all of Philadelphia knew. "British Troops and Ships on the Way," the *Pennsylvania Journal* declared.

The State House spilled over with angry colonists. A congress was called, a gathering set for September, with representatives from all thirteen colonies. Seven distinguished delegates from James's home colony of Virginia were already making plans to attend.

"Glowing patriots, every one," James reported to William Bradford. If only he could be one of them, arguing in the debates, voting on America's future, he thought. All thirteen colonies bonded together as one. James felt a strange new warmth in his soul, all the way home to Virginia.

The time away had done young James good, said Mr. Madison. Perhaps James would settle down and begin learning the family business. But James informed his father that he had no intention of giving his life to a business dependent upon slavery. The Madison plantation required the work of over one hundred African slaves.

However, James added, he just might be interested in buying some of his father's land. Mr. Madison was puzzled. Why would an eldest son wish to spend money for land that he would someday inherit?

3

Drowned Black Rat

In September, James bought two hundred acres of his father's land. He was a landowner. He could vote. He could be elected to public office.

The congress in Philadelphia had made a daring decision. Every town and city, every county in every one of the thirteen colonies was to elect a Committee of Public Safety. If King George would not back down, if there were to be war, the American colonies would be prepared. In December the landowners of Orange County, Virginia, stood outside the court-house to choose the members of their Committee of Public Safety.

The chosen were James's father, nine of his neighbors, and James. James Madison had won his first election. As a committeeman, James roved the county, identifying patriots willing to risk their lives for freedom. He helped his father hand out guns and ammunition from the county's emergency supplies.

In the spring, fighting broke out in the colony of Massachusetts between the colonials and British soldiers. Suddenly, eight Americans lay dead. Eleven more lay bleeding. The Massachusetts citizen army jumped to fifteen thousand. A plea went out to the congress to send a leader. The congress appointed George Washington commander in chief of the new American army. America and Britain were at war.

On April 25, 1776, James proudly waved another certificate of election. The congress had asked the colonies to begin planning for governments of their own. The Virginia lawmakers had called a meeting in Williamsburg. Every county, or section, of Virginia was to send its representatives. James and his uncle William had been elected as delegates from Orange County. Virginia's future was being decided, and he would be one of the decision makers.

Joyfully, James prepared for his first journey to Williamsburg, capital of the colony of Virginia. He would powder his brown hair white for this important occasion, he decided. He would dress in black: black waistcoat and britches, black silk stockings, black shoes with silver buckles, and a high black hat to make him look taller. (James was barely five feet six inches tall. He weighed only one hundred pounds and had a boyish face, even though he was twenty-five years old.) James thought he would look distinguished.

Instead, he arrived at Williamsburg looking like a drowned black rat. The ride on horseback, through drenching spring rains, had made James late. The Virginia Convention had been going on for two days. The tardy newcomer from Orange County slipped into his place. Surrounding him were Virginia's most distinguished statesmen, dressed in jewel-toned velvets and silks.

James yearned to know one representative better, the scholarly Thomas Jefferson. But James was too shy to strike up a conversation.

In fact, shyness washed over James Madison like the swollen, muddy streams he had so recently crossed. The boy from Orange County was a fine whisperer, said Williamsburg's Edmund Randolph, who was even younger than James. But the Princeton graduate spoke with remarkable knowledge of experiments in free government. Soon senior representatives wanted to get a seat beside James Madison.

During official debates, James Madison said not a word. He voted though—for freedom. On May 15, the convention passed a resolution that the Virginia delegates to the Second Continental Congress meeting in Philadelphia declare all thirteen United Colonies free and independent states.

Down came the flag of Great Britain. Up went the flag of Grand Union, proudly waving over Williamsburg. Across the top of the *Virginia Gazette* were the words, "The Thirteen United Colonies. United, We Stand—Divided, We Fall." Virginia was preparing to lead the king's largest American colony, his most glittery jewel, to freedom.

Three and a half weeks later, the Virginia Resolutions for Independence were read before the congress at the Pennsylvania State House. Thomas Jefferson was appointed to write the document that would declare to the king that the colonies no longer intended to obey the laws of Great Britain.

Back in Williamsburg, James Madison was also at work on a document. The Virginia Convention had passed a second resolve to create a Declaration of Rights for the new state of Virginia, a written guarantee of freedoms that could never be taken away from people. James had been assigned to work on the section discussing freedom of religion.

The leader of the discussion, George Mason, made a proposal "that all men should enjoy the fullest toleration in the practice of religion, according to the dictates of conscience." The word *toleration* comes from the Latin *toleratus,* meaning "to bear, to permit." Mason was saying the new government would have the right to decide whether or not the way a Virginian worshipped was acceptable, or tolerable.

The word struck a nerve deep in James Madison. Memories of jailed Baptist preachers flashed across his mind. Should the government have the right to throw a Virginian in jail for worshiping as his heart and mind told him? Not to James Madison's way of thinking. Freedom of worship ought not to be something a government had the privilege of giving or taking away. James thought government and religion ought to be separate.

Quickly, he wrote a revision and passed it to the discussion leader. "Might not toleration be changed to free exercise of religion?" James Madison asked. The wording was changed.

The word change was important. There was more than lawmaking for Virginia at stake during those early summer days of 1776. A new American government was about to be formed. Virginia was preparing to be its model.

The congress in Philadelphia adopted Thomas Jefferson's Declaration of Independence. The United States of America, a brand new nation, was born! The news was proclaimed from the steps of Williamsburg's courthouse. "Huzza! Huzza!" the crowd cried. "Hurray! Hurray!"

James Madison rode home to Orange County, his heart pounding. For the first time in the world, a nation had deliberately declared its freedom. He, James Madison, had changed a word, a word that would make it possible for Americans to believe or disbelieve as their hearts led. He had cast his vote, a vote that led to the declaration of freedom for all Americans. He had made a difference. James knew what to do with his life now. He would be a nation builder.

In January 1778, a year and a half later, James was back in Williamsburg. Independence had been declared, but it had not yet been won. The hard war for freedom dragged on. Patrick Henry had become governor of Virginia. An opening had come up on Governor Henry's council, and James Madison had been elected to fill it.

When James returned to the capital, the first piece of business was a distressing letter from George Washington. The American army, known as the Continentals, was starving. The men were camped for the winter at freezing, snowy Valley Forge, Pennsylvania. The cries of hungry soldiers split the air.

The camp cook had concocted a soup of hogs' bellies, beef bones, and the remaining carrots and potatoes. He'd flavored it with the last of his pepper. Pepper Pot Soup warmed the soldiers' stomachs. It did not fill them, General Washington wrote. He had written dozens of letters to the congress, the worried general continued. No help had come. Might not Virginia lend a hand?

Virginia would take action at once, Governor Patrick Henry declared. It would send 10,000 hogs, 3,000 beef cattle, and 2,600 bushels of salt to preserve the meat. Drats! There would be records to keep, letters to the food suppliers, reports to be filed, the return message to General Washington.

As a speaker, Patrick Henry was as fiery as ever. But he had no patience for writing. He knew someone who did, however, someone whose writing flowed clearly and easily. James Madison was assigned to the writing of government papers.

One morning the governor's new writer failed to appear. He was mysteriously absent the next morning as well. It was so unlike the dependable Madison, Governor Henry mused. Where on earth could he be? Not a councilman knew.

The shopkeepers of Williamsburg knew. The missing Madison had been to each and every one in search of a hat. He'd placed his own in a window, Councilman Madison had insisted. When he'd returned, it was gone. A gentleman, most certainly a gentleman as proper as Mr. Madison, did not appear in public without a hat.

Here came little Madison at last, scurrying to the governor's palace, beneath a hat with a brim as wide as a witch's, the crown no bigger than a pimple. It was the only hat to be had, said the mortified Madison, much to the amusement of the governor and the council.

The next year, Thomas Jefferson became governor of Virginia. The two scholarly Virginians worked side by side. Both Madison and Jefferson loved books and curiosities. Both had a passion for freedom. A warm and lasting friendship began to form.

Governor Jefferson also received a plea from George Washington. The war was going badly, with defeat after defeat for the Americans. The army was marching barefoot. There were no medicines. The congress was soon to meet again in Philadelphia, Washington reminded him. "Please," the worried general begged, "send your ablest and your best."

4

Glowing Patriot

James Madison took his place in the Second Continental Congress on March 20, 1780, four days after his twenty-ninth birthday. His dream had come true. He was one of them, a glowing patriot deciding America's future.

James found himself thrust into a crowd of strangers. He was expected to mingle, he realized in dismay, and to make clever small talk. Shyness snuffed James Madison out like a candle. And in general meetings, when the entire congress gathered for debate, James Madison said not a single word all springtime long.

He listened though. And what did the quiet Madison hear? He heard resentment. States that had sent their assigned money and supplies to the army resented those who had not. He heard arguments, arguments between Maryland and Virginia over who should control the river bordering both states. He heard arguments between New York and New Jersey over duties being charged on bushels of wheat.

He heard self-interest. What concern were the worries of Carolina tobacco growers to a delegate from Massachusetts? His state's worry was the low price fishermen got for a lobster.

Delegate Madison heard fear. The war was going badly. The Americans were losing battle after battle. Suppose British warships were to enter Delaware Bay? Delaware had neither the population nor the money to protect itself.

Money was the biggest problem. Pennsylvania money was not accepted by New Jersey. New Jersey money was not accepted by Pennsylvania. The paper money that the congress had printed was no good anywhere. The congress had no gold or silver to back it up.

The congress could not afford to feed even a single soldier, Madison wrote to Thomas Jefferson. It no longer had the respect of the states. His friend would find the body of once glowing patriots sadly changed.

Madison the thinker thought about the problems of the congress. It had no power to settle arguments between the states. It had no power to collect taxes to support the army. It had no power to set up a unified money system. The congress had practically no power at all.

Madison thought about the problems of the states. "How are things in *your* country?" William Bradford had written during their long-gone college days. Life was depressing in Virginia country, Madison had replied. How were things in Pennsylvania country?

There was the problem. The states did not yet see themselves as parts of a nation greater than themselves. Each state saw itself as its own little country, struggling to survive.

The congress had recently adopted a national emblem, a beautifully decorated banner that proclaimed to the world the goal of the new United States. *E pluribus unum,* declared its Latin motto. "From many, one." The truth of the matter, said James Madison, was that there was no union. America was not yet one nation out of many colonies. It was thirteen separate colonies.

Word got around. Madison had a talent for seeing straight to the heart of a problem. Madison understood. The congress was divided into committees, each one assigned to an area of government. Invitations to speak began dropping into Madison's lap with the abundance of falling leaves. The more James Madison spoke, the more convinced he became that his reason for living was to build the struggling states into a nation.

On October 24, 1781, a messenger sent by General Washington rushed into the State House. The British army had surrendered. The war was over. The delegates gave the exhausted rider a tip from their own money. The congress had no money to give.

The peace treaty was signed in March 1783. King George had lost the largest jewel in his crown. America was free!

But every day at dismissal time, a mob gathered outside the doors of the State House, throwing rocks and shouting insults at the departing delegates. Who were the rock throwers? The soldiers who had won the American Revolution were demanding their pay. The congress fled to Princeton, New Jersey, in shame.

The British looked on and said that the Americans could not manage their country. They thought the Americans would soon be crying to be taken back. Had all the years of war been for nothing? Would America fail? Not if Madison had anything to say about it.

James Madison packed his belongings and returned to Virginia. The time had come for the United States of America to be built into a nation, and James Madison was ready to be one of the builders.

Send books, Madison wrote to his friend Thomas Jefferson. "Send every written word to be found on the histories of nations built from states that were united." Jefferson was living in Paris, serving as America's ambassador to France. There were more bookstores in that city than any other city in the world.

Crates of books arrived at Montpelier, the name given to the Madison home. Tucked in among the reading material was a selection of curiosities for Madison's amusement. A magnifying glass that could be fitted into a cane, a pedometer for counting one's steps, and phosphorescent matches, a magical invention for lighting candles quick as a wink.

Madison studied the books, all two hundred. He read books on politics, and on the histories of nations. There was something about those histories that caused James Madison to take notice. The histories were like Grandmother Madison's stories. They had holes, precious pieces of history lost forever. No one had written them down. As he read, Madison the scholar asked two important questions: Why had governments succeeded? Why had governments failed?

Nations that had failed had been caught up in resentments, arguments, self-interest. Nations that had succeeded had been united by a strong national government. Successful nations had listened to the opinions of the people.

Next, Madison wrote an essay, forty-one pocket-sized pages. (Pocket-sized pages were sure to come in handy for debates.) He described what he had learned about governments from ancient Greece and Rome to Europe in the 1700s. He gave his opinions on what was troubling the American union. The problem, said Madison, was the Articles of Confederation. The guidelines created by congress to hold the colonies together during the war were no more than a loose agreement of friendship. America needed a stronger law of the land.

Last of all, Madison wrote letters, strong, persuasive letters, to Edmund Randolph, then governor of Virginia, and to General George Washington. Tucked into the letters were copies of the essay. Washington's letter held a special request. If a convention of the states were held to revise the Articles of Confederation, would the general attend?

Patrick Henry said he would not attend. He smelled a rat.

5

Something Most Important

George Washington arrived for James Madison's "grand convention of the states" on a Sunday, escorted into Philadelphia by soldiers on high-stepping horses. Cannons boomed. Church bells rang throughout the city. Surely something important was going on, Philadelphians said to one another.

James Madison had slipped into Philadelphia on a workaday Thursday, squeezed into the public coach. He'd checked into Mrs. House's boardinghouse, a block from the State House. No one but the landlady—and old Dr. Franklin sitting under his mulberry tree—took notice.

It was Benjamin Franklin that James Madison had come to see. Dr. Franklin believed in stronger government for the union, too. Madison had arrived on May 3, purposefully early. He had work to do. Franklin had a brand new dining room with a long mahogany table that could seat twenty-four. On May 16, twenty delegates dined at Dr. Franklin's new table. Talks of nation building filled the room.

Madison's job was to get his own Virginia delegation to support the ideas in his essay. Delegates were sure to pay attention to what the largest state had to say. The Virginians met every day, refining their plan.

On the opening day of the convention, Benjamin Franklin arrived at the State House in his Chinese sedan chair, carried by four husky inmates from the Walnut Street Prison. The plump doctor waving cheerily behind the glass windows of his chair, swinging from ten-foot poles, was Philadelphia's favorite curiosity. Something *most* important must be going on, said Philadelphians to one another.

Madison ducked into the State House unnoticed. He chose a chair front and center, which seemed strange. Delegates were used to seeing the quiet Madison buried in the back. James Madison had a reason for such boldness that rainy Friday, May 25, 1787. He needed to be where he could hear every word. Madison planned to take notes and smuggle them out.

Writing down notes was quite proper. An official secretary and others were doing the same. Removing notes from the room was the problem. The delegates had sworn themselves to secrecy so that they could speak their minds freely. Every word written was to be turned in at the end of every session. Not a single newspaper reporter was allowed. But Madison had no thought of leaking the story to the *Pennsylvania Packet,* his favorite newspaper. He had something bigger in mind.

On May 29, Governor Randolph stood up. In his hand was the Virginia Plan, James Madison's plan. Randolph, Virginia's presenter, said he wanted to make the plan perfectly clear. The Virginia Plan was about a strong national government, whose power would be greater than the power of the states.

The room went suddenly still. Randolph was saying that a state could be required to obey a higher central power. The Articles of Confederation said nothing of the kind. The delegates had been called here simply to revise the Articles, had they not? This Virginia Plan was more than a fix-up idea for the Articles of Confederation. It was a totally new kind of government.

What kind of power? the suspicious delegates asked. King George had shown them enough of strong government.

The power of the people, Randolph replied. The national government would be like a tree with three sturdy branches. There would be a legislative branch with representatives of the people to make laws. There would be a judicial branch with courts to interpret the laws. And there would be an executive branch with a president to enforce the laws. The roots of the tree would be firmly planted in democracy.

Immediately, the fifty-five delegates began to ask questions. A president? Would he be like a king? Would all states have an equal vote in the legislature, or would representation there be based on the number of people living in a state? Who would elect the representatives—the landowners? Everybody? Who was everybody?

The questions fast turned into arguments, just as James Madison had known they would. Madison was pleased. Whether they realized or not, the delegates who had gathered in Philadelphia were already involved in considering a new law of the land. There would be no turning back.

Often James Madison jumped into the debate himself. If the new government were to be truly a democracy (a government of the people, for the people, by the people), said Madison, the number of representatives a state had in the legislature ought to be based on its population.

That was all well and good for big states like Virginia, retorted the delegates from the smaller state of New Jersey. They promptly presented an opposing plan. With their plan, New Jersey said, all states would have the same number of representatives. The lawmakers and keepers would have just two new powers, to tax and to regulate trade. Other than that, New Jersey was for sticking with the Articles of Confederation. The states could keep their powers.

The delegates broke out in smiles. The people back home in their states liked having all that power. But leaders such as George Washington, Benjamin Franklin, James Madison, and New York's Alexander Hamilton were concerned. The New Jersey Plan did not give enough attention to the needs of the Union as a whole.

On Tuesday, June 19, the greatest debate of all took place. The time had come to choose between the New Jersey Plan and the Virginia Plan. The delegates saw a new James Madison that Tuesday. His face rosy with conviction, his body alive with energy, Madison walked into the lofty East Room.

The question hung heavy in Philadelphia's hot, humid air. Which would the delegates have? A union standing strong, or thirteen separate hobbling states? Calmly, logically, Madison picked apart the New Jersey Plan sentence by sentence.

Jemmy Madison's voice was no less wispy this June morning of 1787. But the passion and the intensity with which he spoke penetrated Independence Hall. Madison believed in what he was saying, heart and soul.

The vote was cast. The New Jersey Plan was defeated. The United States of America had a plan for a new and powerful law of the land, the Virginia Plan, James Madison's plan. Jemmy Madison sat down and went on with his note taking. Love—love for a nation being united—had conquered shyness.

Far more work needed to be done before the plan could be called a constitution, a well-written law of the land. The delegates worked all summer long trying to reach a balance among the new government's three branches. The delegates wanted to guarantee both freedom and strength for America forever.

James Madison spoke every day. Whenever he was not speaking, he was taking notes. For one hundred days, in his own invented shorthand, James Madison wrote down all that was read and said.

Why did a candle burn far into the night at Mrs. House's window? the curious asked. Madison smiled. He had just been filling in between the lines in his "diary," he replied.

August turned to September. At last the ideas intended to become the law of the nation were ready for the final writing. James Madison was appointed to the five-man Committee of Style and Arrangement. The team of editor-writers went to work.

On September 17, the Constitution of the United States, crisply handwritten on parchment, lay on the table in the East Room. The committee had streamlined a hundred days of wordy philosophy into seven crystal clear Articles. Something important had happened, just as James Madison had planned. The United States of America was about to become truly united.

State by state, the delegates lined up for the signing. Madison placed his name, James Madison Jr., at the bottom of the Virginia delegation. The signers went their separate ways. Madison's diary was tucked away in a drawer.

An urgent new writing job demanded Madison's attention. Alexander Hamilton and a lawyer named John Jay were worried. Politicians were persuading New Yorkers to reject the Constitution.

James Madison was worried too. In order to become the law of the land, the Constitution had to be accepted by the people it would govern. It had to be ratified—formally accepted by the vote of nine of the thirteen states.

Virginia's Governor Randolph had not signed. Neither had several other Virginia delegates. They had to think about it, they said. And there was the outspoken Patrick Henry to worry about. Henry was doing his best to have the document rejected. Would Virginia reject the Constitution? Would other states follow Virginia, the state that had the most people?

Letters signed with the name of an ancient Roman poet began appearing in newspapers. The letters were essays supporting the Constitution. Who was the mysterious Publius? readers wondered. Only the letter writers (Alexander Hamilton, James Madison, and John Jay) knew.

6

Washington Ablaze

Philadelphia in the springtime of 1794 was bursting with newness. Proud new merchant ships laden with silks and China teas filled the harbor. The ships were American: the *George Washington, the Empress of China,* the *Canton.* George Washington, president of the United States of America, sat in Independence Hall. Philadelphia was the nation's new capital.

James Madison was serving in the new Congress. One of his first pieces of business was to present a Bill of Rights, a written guarantee of individual rights for Americans, to be added to the Constitution. When Congressman Madison walked the cobblestone streets, Philadelphians took notice. There went the "Great Little Madison," they said, the Father of the Constitution. Many heads had fathered the Constitution, said modest James Madison. He had merely worked behind the scenes.

But there was one Philadelphian that Congressman Madison very much wished would notice him. Her name was Dolley Payne Todd. The charming Dolley was just twenty-five years old and quite pretty. James Madison was forty-three and brushing his hair to cover a bald spot. Dolley knew just how to make the quiet bachelor feel completely at ease. In September they were married.

When Thomas Jefferson became the nation's third president, he chose James Madison to be his secretary of state. Together they arranged the purchase of the Louisiana Territory from France. The Louisiana Purchase added all lands south of Canada and north of Mexico, from the Mississippi River west to the Rocky Mountains. The United States became eight hundred thousand square miles bigger. As Jefferson's second term as president came to a close, he hoped Madison would be elected to take his place.

On March 4, 1809, James Madison placed his hand on the Bible and solemnly swore to preserve, protect, and defend the Constitution of the United States.

Schoolmaster Robertson's tongue-tied scholar had just become the fourth president of the nation.

President Madison's ten-minute inaugural speech was serious. The United States and Great Britain were on the brink of war. The British had been in a long war with France. British sailors were seizing cargo from American ships bound for French ports. They were kidnapping American sailors, claiming that the Americans were subjects of the king, and forcing them to fight for the British navy.

Subjects of the king indeed! America was no longer a little string of colonies belonging to King George. It was a nation. The United States had the Constitution. Congress had the power to support an army and a navy. American warships, like the U.S.S. *Constitution,* were the fastest in the world. The president had the power to lead.

President Madison did all in his power to avoid leading the young nation into war. He put a stop to trade with Britain. But the British went right on snatching American sailors.

According to the Constitution, it was the president's responsibility to send periodic reports to Congress on how things were going for the Union. Should there be problems, it was the president's responsibility to recommend necessary action. In November 1811,

President Madison sent a grim report. America must prepare for the possibility of war.

Madison sent a warning of America's war preparations to England by ship. Americans hoped for a peaceful settlement. The ship returned with bad news. The British had no change of mind. One June 18, 1812, the United States declared war on Britain.

Lines of British warships patrolled America's Atlantic coast. American fishermen and merchants were stuck in their ports. It was all due to "Mr. Madison's war," New Englanders said. There was talk of Connecticut and Massachusetts actually leaving the United States and even talk of removing Madison from the presidency. The insults were actually quite healthy, President Madison said. It showed the citizens understood the freedom of speech guaranteed by the Bill of Rights he had worked so hard for when he was a congressman.

On August 17, 1814, fifty British warships anchored at the mouth of the Patuxent River, southeast of Washington, D.C. Four thousand British soldiers, called redcoats, were aboard.

Washington was the nation's capital. Those four thousand redcoats were entirely too close. President Madison used his constitutional power to protect the nation and ordered up the Maryland and Virginia militias (groups of citizens trained to fight during emergencies). He wanted America's official documents moved to safety.

Did Dolley have the courage to remain at the presidential mansion for a couple of days and see to the packing of the nation's papers? Madison asked. And his personal papers tucked away in drawers, would she see to those as well? He felt that his duty as commander in chief of the army was to go to the American troops.

Dolley replied that her only fear was for her husband's safety. The papers would be packed. Left in the President's House with only a few servants, Dolley packed papers (four trunks full). Then she called for a carriage. At midnight on August 23, a messenger dashed to the President's House. The British were on full march to the capital. The papers, America's story, had gone in the carriage to safety just in time.

The next day, Wednesday, August 24, Dolley ordered the table to be set for President Madison's three o'clock dinner, just as she always had. But shortly before three o'clock, a man appeared, frantically waving his hat. He had an urgent message from the president. Clear out! Clear out! he cried. The British were coming. Dolley jumped into her carriage with her housemaid Sukey. A driver whisked them to nearby Georgetown.

In the black of night, British soldiers stole into the President's House. The redcoats seated themselves at President Madison's dinner table. They jokingly made a toast to the health of James Madison, raising the crystal wine glasses.

When they left, the order was given to torch the President's House. By morning, nothing remained but four charred walls. The building where Congress met was also burned. A question hung heavy in the capital's smoke-choked air. Would the American nation stand strong? Or would it fall to the British?

The British were already claiming victory. "The proud seat of the traitors has been destroyed," London newspapers announced. President Madison issued a proclamation, calling on " all the good people of the United States to unite in their hearts and hands."

Fresh volunteers filled the American army and navy. After a hard-fought battle, the Americans defeated the British in the nearby city of Baltimore. Everyone hoped for victory at the upcoming battle at New Orleans on the seacoast of Louisiana. News of victory came in early February. The British who had survived the battle at New Orleans were headed out to sea.

Valentines Day 1815 was a day of jubilation for the United States. A messenger bearing an official-looking envelope arrived at the temporary presidential mansion. He was escorted to the second floor, where the president and his cabinet were meeting. The British had surrendered. The country was at peace.

"I played *The President's March* on the violin," Paul Jennings, the president's personal servant later wrote. "We all went crazy with joy." President Madison had led the nation through its first crucial test. United, America would stand.

Was there anything in the world that could make President Madison's joy more complete? Just one. Nearing the end of his eight-year presidency, James Madison found himself longing for Montpelier.

7

The Diary

Montpelier clattered with chatter, throbbed with a hundred guests elbowing their way to the dining room's bountiful buffet. Dolley had flung wide the doors to the new back porch, sweet with jasmine and roses. The Madisons were throwing a party.

The president was nowhere to be seen. He had slipped away to his library. President Madison was still not much for crowds. He treasured precious moments of quiet, poring over a favorite book.

He had time for reading, time for measuring rainfall in the tin cup he kept by Montpelier's front gate. There was time for peering through the spyglass in hopes of discovering a carriage of nieces and nephews coming to visit Uncle James. President Madison had many nieces and nephews.

On rainy days, the president's young visitors might make themselves cozy in his upstairs library, which was crammed from floor to ceiling with four thousand books. Uncle James actually owned that many books! Rainy days were for reading. Uncle James read aloud from *The Spectator.* Perhaps a niece or nephew might be inspired to become a thinker!

If the day were fair, the young visitors might wander to the stables with sugar cubes for Liberty, Uncle's favorite horse. Uncle James told wonderful horse stories, such as the one about the time he misplaced a horse in Williamsburg.

It happened during his days as a writer for Patrick Henry, Madison would begin. The children's eyebrows would go up. Their brilliant uncle, "Father of the Constitution," had actually forgotten where he put his horse?

But the story James Madison most wanted America's future thinkers to remember was the story of their Constitution, the story in the diary tucked away in a drawer. Week after week, month after month, President Madison labored over the hundred day's story, in writing no bigger than a redbird's scratch.

On July 6, 1826, President Madison's work was interrupted by sad news. His friend Thomas Jefferson had died two days ago, on the fiftieth anniversary of the Declaration of Independence. John Adams, the nation's second president, had died on the same day. Jefferson was gone. Adams and Washington were gone. James Madison was the only one of America's Founding Fathers still alive. It was more important than ever that he tell the story of all that had happened in Philadelphia so long ago.

President Madison was growing old himself. Often his seventy-five-year-old hands were so swollen and painful with arthritis that he could not write. Then Dolley's hands became his hands. It was a tedious business, she said, transcribing the long ago Philadelphia story. Madison wanted nothing left out. Every speech, every outburst, every little joke, must be remembered.

On an autumn afternoon in 1834, the eighty-three year old James Madison informed Dolley that his writing project was for the people of the United States after he died. Dolley's eyes filled with tears.

For the last six months of his life, President Madison was too crippled up to get out of bed. Dolley fixed him a bed-sitting room across from Montpelier's dining room. That way, he could join in the conversation.

By June 1836, President Madison's doctor realized that his patient's tired body could not go on much longer. Would Madison like to be given stimulants so he could die on the fourth of July as had Jefferson and Adams? the doctor asked

It mattered not that Americans remember the day of his departure from this world, the Father of the Constitution replied. However, he did have a final message to his nation:

"The advice nearest to my heart and deepest in my convictions is that the Union of the states be cherished and perpetuated."

James Madison died on June 28, 1836. Family, friends, and one hundred Montpelier slaves accompanied him to his resting spot, footsteps from the spot where Grandmother's old house had stood. Madison's account of the creation of the Constitution was purchased by the United States government and is in the Library of Congress. It is the most complete record in existence of the story of the Constitution of the United States of America, a story without holes. Madison had managed to include even his own speeches, all 164 of them, designated as having been delivered by "Mr. M."

Selected Bibliography

Bowen, Katherine Drinker. *Miracle at Philadelphia: The Story of the Constitutional Convention May to September 1781.* Boston: Little Brown and Company, 1986.

Earle, Alice Morse. *Home Life in Colonial Times.* Stockbridge, MA: The Berkshire Traveler Press, 1974.

Geier, Clarence R., and Reeves, Matthew. "JMU and Montpelier Archaeology Reconstructs Early Madison Record." *Montpelier: James Madison University Magazine* 24, no. 2 (Spring 2001): 49–57.

Hakim, Jay. *A History of the US: From Colonies to Country.* New York: Oxford University Press, 1993.

Ketcham, Ralph. *James Madison: A Biography.* Charlottesville, VA: University of Virginia Press, 1990.

Rakove, Jack N. *Madison: Writings.* New York: Literary Classics of the United States, 1999.

Websites

www.montpelier.org
James Madison's Montpelier. This site is a welcome to Montpelier, lifelong home of James Madison.

www.jamesmadisonmuseum.org
The James Madison Museum. This site takes you to the James Madison Museum in Orange, Virginia.

Index

About the Author

Barbara Mitchell is a frequent visitor to James Madison's Montpelier. Like Mr. Madison, Barbara was a quiet child, a lover of books, and traces her fascination with history to stories her grandmother told.

When not writing stories of her own, Barbara especially enjoys ringing handbells with the Chancel Ringers, whose director is known to encourage, "LOUDER, BARB."

Ms. Mitchell lives in Wilmington, Delaware with her husband and ten-year-old granddaughter. This is her tenth biography for young readers.